Kintsugi

Whispers from the Golden

Seams

Tales of a Mended Vessel

Victoria Swindle

ISBN: 9781676031482

DEDICATION

This book is dedicated to my mother, Elvira, who never gave up on
me. Despite all I went through and subjected myself to, and the
number of years I wallowed in the mess I made, she continued to
love, care and pray from me. She is truly a priceless jewel.

To all of the abused and addicted, family members and friends that
witness(ed) the struggles, and people in the community that hear the
rumors and tales told; this is a portion of my testimony I am sharing
to allow a brief glimpse into portions of my past so you can see
where the Lord brought me to be in my present. I share these
experiences with you so you can know no matter how many times
you have been knocked down, how many pieces you feel you have
been broken into, or how utterly lost and beyond repair you may feel
you are, God has a way of mending your pieces; to not only make
you whole again, but to make you more beautiful than ever before!

CONTENTS

PREFACE

During my preparation for writing this book I was reminded of Isaiah 64:8 (NLT), "But now LORD, you are our Father. We are the clay, and you are our potter. All of us are the works of your hand." I was also reminded of Jeremiah 18:3-6 (NLT), "So I did as he told me and found the potter working at his wheel. But the jar he was making did not turn out as he had hoped, so he crushed it into a lump of clay and started over. Then, the Lord gave me this message: "O Israel, can I not do to you as this potter has done to his clay? As the clay is in the potter's hand, so are you in my hand."

Just as the potter sometimes must crush the clay and reshape it, God reshapes us throughout our lives. We endure trials and tribulations along the way, finding ourselves tried and hardened by the fires of life. At certain points in time as we mature, we find ourselves broken. Not knowing how to pick up the pieces. Not knowing how to become whole again. In some instances, we stay broken for so long, we forget what being whole is. Even more saddening, there are those of us who have never experienced wholeness because we have been broken our entire lives.

As I continued to pray over the content of this book, I was reminded of an ancient Japanese practice called kintsugi, which means to join with gold. In this practice, each vessel is regarded as highly valuable because of the time and care put into each hand-crafted piece and the uniqueness that is birthed from the process. Just like the fingerprints of human beings, each one is unique in and of itself. With the pieces being so valuable, the belief was adopted that when clay vessels are broken the pieces should not be discarded as if they any less valuable. Instead, they should be delicately retrieved and pieced back together using gold resin. This process of mending with gold, kintsugi, not only mends the vessels; it adds to the value of the them and helps to tell visually intricate and unique stories of how each vessel was once broken but was made whole and functional again.

When I meditated on this practice of kintsugi I was in awe thinking of how our Father God gently picks up our broken pieces when we finally surrender ourselves to Him and mends us back together delicately; just like the art of kintsugi. Everything He created is of great value. Especially His children. And it is His Holy Spirit that serves as the gold resin and seals the bonds between the cracks of our broken pieces. One by one, piece by piece, detail by intricate detail, the potter mends his broken vessels with the bonding of His priceless Holy Spirit.

The beautiful lines in the cracks whisper softly the stories of the trials we have faced and the pains we have endured in our broken states. The soft bulging of the golden lines give light to how we were delicately pressed, piece by piece, to be reconstructed into who the Lord intended us to be; a testimony to His saving grace and timeless limitless ability to heal. Suddenly, we find that are whole again. Uniquely flawed. Yet more beautiful, precious, and   valuable   than   ever   before. ☐

ONE NIGHT...MY HAIR

The night began just like any other. The tattoos had been done; the music had been turned down to more of a conversive background volume from the usual resounding party volume of the business day. The drinks were turned up, the snow was consumed, and the after party had begun to wind down.

I still don't remember what the argument was about. But I do remember the fight. Most times it was about petty nothingness anyway. People get cranky when the dope runs out. Consequently, arguments and sometimes fights ensue. So, there we were. I have no idea who went in first. But I remember tousling around the main floor of the tattoo shop, screaming at him to stop; as usual. But that was the thing. Once he got into a fit of rage while he was high, there was no stopping. There was only tiring. Eventually, he would tire; as usual. That much I knew for sure.

I tried my best to hold my own; as usual. But that darned glass coffee table just HAD to be in the middle of the floor. And who gets slung into the middle of the glass table? Ding, ding, ding, ding, ding! We have a winner! The glass table champion is...dun dun dunnnnn...Vykkiiii!!!

God knows that hurt. Stunned the crap out of me. Back

hurt. Shoulders hurt. Head hurt. My goodness, my head hurt. At least it was "safety" glass. That could've been nasty. But since I didn't die from impalement by glass, I thought, 'Maybe I can shake this off. It hurts, but I've got to move. Right? That's a cardinal rule of fighting. Keep moving.' Then, before I could even begin to shake... 'My hair! Whyyyy my hairrrruh? OMG!!! SERIOUSLY?!?!?! NOT MY HAIRRRR!!!'

How, at 6' 2" tall and 175 lbs. does one get dragged by the hair of their head? Well, I learned that night that's what a man that's 5' 6" tall and 135 lbs. soaking wet is capable of when he's hopped up on cocaine. So, across the floor I went. Over the broken table pieces and through the broken glass... Jesus! My arms, my back and my legs felt like they were being shredded to pieces. All the while I'm screaming, "Stop! Help! Somebody help me," As I was dragged a few feet at a time across the room; each tug sending a fresh shot of pain down from my head into my shoulders. I looked around desperately pleading as our "friends" cowered back on the sofas and chairs watching in disbelief, shame, and sad disappointment. They wouldn't because they felt they couldn't. Regardless of what year it was, we were in Mississippi baby. And one of those old-school backwoods unwritten country laws is, you don't come between a man and his business with his wife. I don't care who you are or how badly he's dogging her. You just DON'T. PERIOD.

When my involuntary movement ceased, my hair had helped deliver me to my destination for the night. There I was on the cold concrete patio just outside the back door, and he was closing the door on me. With the little fight I had left, I pushed back. I pushed and screamed and screamed and pushed; to no avail, of course. So, yeah. He won. And the door slammed. And there I lay; sobbing uncontrollably; cursing and banging on the door and yelling until I had no voice left. And to what end? So, the coyotes could hear? A black bear or bobcat maybe? I don't know. Maybe the wild hogs or the rats in the potato field in the next property over would care, or the deer in the forest at the hunting club that surrounded us on the other three sides. Maybe even the little fishes in the stocked pond at the far end of our three-acre lot could have compassion on my desperate cries. The critters may have heard, but there was no help. Period. The funny part is, he turned up the volume on the music, so they didn't have to hear me outside wailing. How about THEM apples? Ha! What a guy!!!

And man, nobody will ever know how many times I thought about going to visit those little fishes at the bottom of the pond that night, knowing I can't swim. I don't even know how many times I pondered it, or how long. But since there were water moccasins, timber rattlers, and cane brake rattlers around, I figured between the walk back through the overgrown brush and the dive in, it wouldn't take long to die anyway. A combination of snake bite and drowning would've been like hitting the jackpot the way I was feeling. But nah I couldn't. I just couldn't.

When I think of it now, I remember the thoughts of leaving my children behind are what kept me from stirring up snakes and walking into the lake that night. I couldn't leave them in misery and trauma. Not like that. And I most certainly couldn't leave them with their dad. Not saying I was much better off than him at the time. But at the time I also liked to believe I was the saner one in the home.

My phone was in the house, so there was no calling anyone. In trying to rationalize I knew there was absolutely no way I was walking in the dark down that old country road in the rain during a thunderstorm. Especially not bloodied and bruised. Our nearest neighbor was almost an entire mile away, and there were too many wild animals that might just decide to try me as a snack in my already battered and defeated state. Nah. I would just stay put on the cold concrete slab that made up the back patio of our quaint little house, listening to the rain pour down, the thunder roll, and the lightening crashing down; praying no lightning bolt got as close to me as the one did when it struck the tree beside me that time when I was a teenager. Hopefully. Prayerfully. God, I was so scared. Outside. Alone. Hurt. Bleeding. Bruised. Picking through my head, crying as I discovered clump after clump shedding from where he had dragged me out.

Then, a ray of sunshine came from the dark. In all that commotion I had forgotten something. I had a companion after all. My baby. My doggie. My Tattoo. Yes, Tattoo was his name. And that night he brought me solace; more than any of my so-called friends, and most certainly more than the one who vowed so many years before to be my love and my protector. Yeah, Tattoo brought me comfort and warmth. So that night I slept on the porch with my doggie.

THE SAGA OF THE FRONT DESK CLERK – ACT 1

Ben came by the apartment, excited as he could be asking for Danny. Ben had news. Good news; and he couldn't wait to share. "Where's bruh?" he asked. "He's in the studio. Come on," I replied. Into the studio we went. There, our dear friend shared all his excitement with us. "They are opening a tattoo shop on Main Street. The owner was asking about artists in the area because she doesn't run ink. But she is looking for an artist to bring in because her original guy didn't work out. I told her about you and let her see my ink. Bruh, she wants to see you ASAP," he explained eagerly. Danny replied, "How soon does she want to see me?" Our friend said, "She's waiting on you now. I told her you lived just down the street, and that I would come pick you up and bring you to her." "Oh," Danny said, "Give me a minute to grab my stuff." He packed up his trusty tattoo bag along with his portfolio pics, and off they went.

Myself, along with my swollen baby belly and two older boys, said our goodbyes and gave well wishes as they exited the apartment. I was pretty far along; six months in, and we were excited about welcoming son number three.

A couple of hours later, Danny walked in full of

excitement. He explained that the shop was A-1 and so was the equipment. He no longer had to work with his old equipment and the terms of their payment contract was ideal for an artist of his caliber. Also, there was a front desk clerk that was very knowledgeable about the business, and she would be handling all the money and paperwork for the shop. Becky. She was best friend to the shop owner. But they were both cool and excited about working with him.

The next day, I went down with him per invite to meet his new crew. Everyone seemed cool, but there was something about the front desk clerk that didn't sit well with me. I told him they seemed a bit sketchy; Becky, especially so. He went on to explain they were cool and did no more than we did in our recreational time; some blow here, some drinking there, some pills here, some meth there. The usual for us both while I wasn't on pregnancy hiatus. Still, there was something about that chick that just didn't sit right with me. I would later find out why.

Danny went to work, day after day, excited to finally be in a shop instead of working from home. With all our old habits, we had never gotten up the money to invest in a brick and mortar location. In hindsight, if we hadn't been such drunks and druggies, we could have had a very successful art business. But, that's life. You live and you learn. Right?

He would come home for lunch to check on me and the boys since I had been placed on bed rest. Then, in the evening after work, he would come in and tell me about the adventures of the day and the beautiful artistic custom pieces he had done. It was great, other than being on bed rest.

They started out as good times, as we defined them back then. Then, word started coming to me that Danny and Becky had a "thing" going on. That they would sneak off together getting high, and that sometimes he'd be so zooted he couldn't work. People were beginning to complain about him stepping out in the middle of a tattoo and returning sketched out. It was no secret that getting high was a "thing". But now he was becoming unreliable, and our friends hated her because they all knew me and knew that I was pregnant, and she was trying to impose.

The entire neighborhood was in an uproar about them; the Danny and Becky thing; and how they were so low down for doing what they were doing, knowing full well I was already home trying to care for two small boys while I was supposed to be on bed rest. Still, they did what they did. Me personally, at the time, my philosophy was whatever with Becky. She doesn't have this ring and she never will. Danny pays these bills and he comes home at night to me. That's all that matters. Dummy. Not realizing what everyone else was seeing at the time; I deserved more.

I was a great wife to Danny. That, I refuse to deny myself. There were all too many instances in which his homeboys and clients would kindly remind him of that; some even issued it as a warning to be careful of how he treated me because there were others waiting for the day I walked away.

Despite all his shortcomings, or how many times he had cheated with young white chicks in the past, I never retaliated. I raised hell; yes. But revenge cheating was a no. Not even with all the advances of other men, and even some of his so-called friends. Cheating was a no for me. I just couldn't bring myself to it. Now, I thank God for allowing me to have that mentality, even in my times of heartbreak. Now, I understand the fullness of being repaid what you give, and that is a debt I am glad I do not have to repay or answer for.

Still, Danny and Becky did their thing. I would

sometimes show up to the shop unannounced; occasionally with my two youngsters in tow, just to see what the haps were. I remember once, my cousin and bestie, Tasha, flew into my apartment in a rage. "Girl, you better come get this motherfucker! Your husband down here whoring at the shop is one thing. But now he's got my husband down there with him in that shit talking to white bitches, hanging out, getting high and shit. I will go turn that motherfucker out." So, off we went. Seven months pregnant and supposed to be on bed rest; but to the shop I went.

There they were, congregated like a bunch of skittish antelope behind the glass-front of the establishment. All high as kites. Tattoo shop full. And not one person was there for business. Everyone was there "chilling'" getting high and flirting. We sat in the car on the street for a moment to observe. Sadly, they were all so gone they didn't even notice.

Tasha jumped out of the vehicle, no longer able to contain herself. She slung the glass door open and ran up on her husband, pointing her finger in his face and issuing promises of a well-whooped behind along with threats of a divorce. He, as usual, cursed and yelled back. But Danny, like he was so accustomed to doing, stood there looking like a deer in the headlights. There was no use of me saying anything to him, nor him to me. He already knew what the business was. I despised him for this public humiliation, and he knew it. Sadly, though his face and temperament showed remorse, it was like he was unable to stop himself. I knew it and so did he. He had a serious problem. But, if he was paying the bills and coming home at night, he was just doing what men do. Right?

Finally, the shop owner emerged from her hiding place upstairs. She was irate at the commotion that had been brought there, disturbing her peace and that of her establishment. Well, really, we were killing her high. Still, she wasn't happy and threatened to call the police. That night, Tasha and her husband were banned from the shop and I was asked not to bring back anymore "bad" company. This pissed me off to the fullest because I knew they just wanted me to go so they could facilitate the affair that was going on between Danny and Becky. But it was cool if he was paying the bills and coming home at night. Right?

Then, one night, he didn't come home. There was no late-night party or early morning 3AM arrival. The sun came up and my then husband was nowhere to be found. That was the straw that broke the camel's back. Just not in the way one would think. I had dealt with public humiliation on a level which most could NEVER fathom. But this... 'This ish right here nigga?' This was a whole other level of disrespect. I never wanted to play the game. But this. This was grounds for retaliation. I refused to become a cheating wife. But I would have my vengeance. No question about it. The game was officially on and I would, without a doubt, be the victor.

Later that day, just after lunch, he finally arrived. As he entered the apartment, I could hear him coming down the hallway in slow motion. I could feel his heaviness and dis-ease as he came down the hallway and approached the bedroom door. Finally, he stood in the doorway looking lost, heavily burdened, and hurt.

"Babe, I'm so sorry," he said. I refused to speak. I only stared at him with anger burning in my eyes. I was livid, and he knew it. He approached the bedside where I lay and reached for my hand. "Babe, I'm so sorry," he repeated coming to tears. "Please babe. Kluklietzamu," which was his pet name and deepest term of endearment for me, "Please forgive me."

All I could do was stare at him. I wanted to hit him on the face so badly. I wanted to kick him in the chest so hard. There were many things I wanted to do to him. Many things. But to what avail? And as much as I wanted to curse him out and let him have every piece of my mind, I knew it would only add to the chaos that was already abounding and he would run away and shut down. So, I took a few cleansing breaths and allowed the more "rational" me to take control.

"Babe I'm so sorry," he continued. Finally, I broke my silence, "For what? What exactly are you sorry for?" His answer took me aback and infuriated me even more, "I don't know." Me, "What?" Him, "I don't know. That's just it. I don't know." At this I sat up on the side of the bed, swollen feet dangling; baby belly protruding over my thighs, "You mean to tell me you were gone all night, just coming home after lunch, and you don't know what you're sorry for?" He replied, "No. I don't. I know I'm wrong for staying out. I'm wrong for not coming home. But I don't know what happened." All the while, he was on his knees crying his eyes out.

My knees were wet with Danny's tears. I had never seen him so distraught. Never. He went on to try to explain, "I asked if anyone had a pain pill I could take for my back. Becky said she had a Lortab. She handed it to me, and I popped it. Next thing I know I'm waking up in her bed. Babe, I promise you I don't know what happened. The entire night was a blur. I remember getting in her car because she was going to bring me home. Next thing I remember, I was in a bathtub and someone was bathing me; running water over my locs. And there was a giant window over the tub. I remember a round tub. Then, there were tall wooden bed posts. The next thing I know I wake up in this whore's bed. I don't know what I've done babe.

All I know is it's bad and I don't know if you'll ever forgive me." I listened carefully as he attempted to piece together the events that had unfolded the night before. Still, I felt no sorrow for him. It was his irresponsible actions that landed him in that position.

This sent me into a level of rage I didn't know I could achieve. And, once again, I felt my anxiety kicking in. An attack was on its way, but I knew I had to get it under control immediately or my contractions would begin again. The doctors already had me on bed rest and taking breathaline pills to stop pre-term contractions due to stress. I closed my eyes and tried to focus on my breathing; calm, gentle, breathing as he lay on my knees crying uncontrollably.

When I was finally able to contain myself, I worked on attempting to understand what I had just heard. He walked through, step by step, trying to recall the events that had occurred the night before. Each time, he was only able to regurgitate the bits and pieces he had previously mentioned. In all honesty, with the state he was in and the way things had happened, I refused to believe him. There was no way I could believe him. This was just his way of delivering yet another sob story in an attempt for me to forgive him. This time though, it wasn't going to work.

"Man, get the fuck out of here with that bullshit," I said very calmly and very low. He stopped and looked up at me. Stunned by my response he asked, "What?" "I said get the FUCK out of HERE with that BULLshit," I said again calmly and low but very accentuated; carefully stressing my syllables in case he missed anything. "If you think I'm going to believe this bullshit you're coming here with after you've been fucking around with that whore in plain sight all this time, you have SERIOUSLY got me fucked up. I need you to take them funky assed lies and them fake assed tears and get the FUCK out my face," looking down at him intently, "...now."

Danny looked at me in disbelief, "But babe, I'm serious. I really don't know." His face was full of shock, disbelief, and disgust, as if he were hurt to his core because I didn't receive his explanation. "GET THE FUCK OUT!" I yelled in his face. I had completely lost my resolve. It was gone; out the window; and there was no coming back. "Piece of shit assed nigga. Fucking around with this white bitch and then gonna come here bringing me these bullshit assed tears like it's gonna make me believe or forgive your punk ass. GET THE FUCK OUT!" He rose from his knees and looked at me with the eyes of someone that knew they were dead wrong, but was confused about what had happened. He dropped his head and repeated, "I'm so sorry babe," as he walked out.

☐

POST-PARTUM

We had recently moved to the Acres. We chose a two-bedroom mobile home tucked away in a little corner of the superb. We couldn't get anything too expensive with the new baby. Still, we were glad and grateful we had managed to move out of the apartment soon after we learned it was infested with black mold. At the time, our oldest was four and our second bundle of joy had recently made his grand entrance. Business was picking up in the small city of Tupelo, Mississippi, and we were excited about life there with our little family.

Still, there were adjustments to be made. We had just moved, and I was only a week or so post-partum. This meant I would need to continue to rest. But how could I when the house still needed to be set up from the move? The business was just taking off, and since this place was all we could afford at the time, the living room was the tattoo studio. With the influx of new clientele, there was an almost constant flow of clients. I had no time to sit still. I had to see to our clients and to the children to be sure our home and operations flowed as smoothly as possible.

My parents insisted and so did his; I needed to get some rest and spend time bonding with the children. Once I finally agreed, my dear sweet hubby drove me to Alabama to my parent's house where my mother would care for me and help me with the baby until my six-week resting period was up. My parents were so excited to see me. And to be honest, once I arrived and kicked my feet up, I was relieved to be able to finally get some rest.

For some odd reason, around the third day at my parent's place I started getting a funky feeling in my gut. I called my husband, asked how things were going, and explained that I didn't feel right. He said everything was cool and tried to ease my concern. Still, I just couldn't get settled in my spirit. Something wasn't right. He was hiding something, and I knew it. So, I approached my mother with all the sincerity I could and asked if she and my dad would take me home. She insisted I try to remain calm and relax. But I just couldn't. I had to get home. Something wasn't right in my house.

Finally, my parents agreed to take me home. We left for Tupelo the following afternoon and arrived around dusk. As we entered the driveway, I noticed a vehicle parked there that was not familiar. I'd had time to grow accustomed to our regular clients and friends' vehicles, and this was neither. As I got out of the car, out walked the hubby. He met me at the door looking shocked and asked what I was doing there. Well, of course I responded with the smart remark, "I live here. That's what I'm doing here. You are hiding something, and I want to see what's going on." No sooner than I said this a young white chick came to the door.

I guess we all know how this goes. Right? He looked at me, then looked at her, then back at me. "Babe, this isn't what it looks like. She's a new tattoo client, and we were discussing a new tattoo." I replied, "But she is in my house. Alone with my husband. Unaccompanied. We both know that's not how this goes." The agreement was, no women at the house while he's alone, and no men in the house while I was alone. Not because we didn't trust each other, but out of respect. This was the agreement that had been established well beforehand when the business first kicked off. "But babe, she's just a client," he said nervously while she stood in the doorway looking like a deer in the headlights. "So, you expect me to believe she is just a client, but she's standing in the door looking like the cat that swallowed the canary, and now is afraid for her life. Okay."

A heated argument ensued. Of course, I was irate. But when he asked me to let her leave, I did; hesitantly, with my fists balled up, standing very near the door so she could feel the heat from my breath as she passed through the threshold. But... I did. I let her go. And as I walked into the house, my gaze fell on the coffee table. On this coffee table, gleaming like the morning sun was a stack of four Magnums. Yeah. You guessed it. I went off.

I ran to the door, but to no avail. She must've realized their folly because she spun out of the driveway; kicking rocks as her tires dug into the gravel. And him. He had every excuse as to why there were condoms on the living room table. All the way down to them belonging to his homeboy that had left them there. When it comes to this lady, I can say my parents raised a lot of things. But a fool isn't one of them.

And to think, I just gave birth to his first-born seed. Instead of joyfully celebrating his wife and new son, he felt it was okay to bring another woman into our home to screw around with while I was in another state caring for our new baby and being cared for by my mother. 'How low down can you be?' were my thoughts. Even if he didn't have sex with her, it was very clear that that was the plan. That, within itself, was enough to go Ham about.

18

I didn't want to hurt him though. I just wanted him to hurt as much as he had hurt me. So, that day was the very first day I can remember cursing him like a rabid dog. It was also the first time I destroyed his equipment. Tattoo equipment, speakers, keyboards, everything I could get my hands on I threw, smashed into the walls, or stomped on. Sad to say, it wouldn't be the last time I destroyed his things, and it was the beginning of the end of our wedded bliss.

THE SAGA OF THE FRONT DESK CLERK – ACT 2

After Danny left, I broke down in tears, crying uncontrollably. I have no idea how long it lasted. I do remember I eventually cried myself to sleep. When I woke, he was back. But he wasn't alone. He was standing near the bed, but like the intelligent man he was, he stood back at a safe distance. He knew that after I reached a certain point of anger, I tended to throw things; sometimes at him instead of the walls. At this point in our relationship, the fighting had grown to be much more than simple arguments and cursing.

Physical altercations had become a part of life. Given with my pregnant state, my temperament, and the present circumstances, he knew I was completely unpredictable. There was no telling what I would do. With me holding my composure as well as I had done after he had arrived home from his night of absence, he was nervous. He knew I could snap at any moment, and he wasn't sure what the consequences would be behind that level of betrayal. At that point, we had been together five years. Within those five, there was never a night he didn't come home. Late nights? Yes. Early mornings? Yes. But never had the sun come up on him being absent before.

I'll never forget how he asked that night before he went to bed, "Is it safe for me to go to sleep?" I just laughed and said, "Yeah, if you think so," then turned over laughing to myself; amused by the thoughts running through my head.

I awoke to Danny's voice softly calling me, "Babe. Hey babe. I'm home." Then a pause. Then, "Babe, I'm sorry. I know you're resting, but I need you to wake up. I have someone here that wants to talk to you. Please don't be too mad. He just wants to talk to you for a minute."

Me being me at the time, he was not in a good place. My thoughts were as follows; 'Firstly, I'm pregnant. Very pregnant. Secondly, I just finished crying myself to sleep over you. Thirdly, I'm angrier than you could ever imagine a human being is capable of being. Fourthly, I'm fighting to keep my contractions down because I do NOT want to lose this baby. Fifthly, I don't want to hear a motherfucking thing YOU or any of your friends have to say.' Those were my thoughts.

As I slid up in the bed, still groggy from my nap, I whispered, "Who is it, and what the FUCK do they want?" Yeah, my mouth was terrible. At that point in my life, the Hoover Dam couldn't hold back the waterfall of foul language that poured from me on the daily. Especially not at times like these.

He replied, "It's Ben. He wants to talk to you." I gave him a burning side-eye. He knew who to bring to rationalize with me. If I didn't listen to anyone else, I would listen to Ben. We were brother and sister from different mothers and fathers. We were of no relation whatsoever. Still, Ben was my brother. And I was his sister. And, to this day, no one in the world can say otherwise without stern objection and swift correction. I love my brother and he loves me. Period. He also loved Danny and would move the world for either of us. So, it pained him to bear witness to the things that were happening between us.

Hesitantly, I finally said, "I'm coming. Let me put some clothes on." Taking my time, I made myself decent and presentable for my company. I knew this wasn't going to be a short conversation. I already knew what he was there for, and nothing about it was simple. I made my way down the hallway rubbing my face to wake as best I could and try to hide the complete and total utter disgust I had at the time for my then husband.

I sat and looked at Ben. Ben looked at me. He saw the hurt in my eyes, then looked at Danny. He rolled his eyes at Danny, then shook his head. He dropped his head for a moment, then proceeded to ask one of the craziest questions he could at the moment, "How ya doing Sis?" I looked at him and let out a chuckle, along with a sly sideways grin, "Oh I'm good," cutting my glare to Danny, who sat across the room in our large Lazy Boy looking like a down-trodden animal that had been abandoned and left to its own demise. Ben continued, "Good. You look good. Glad to see you're holding it together, given the circumstances." Then there was the awkward silence.

"So," Ben said hesitantly as he broke the uncomfortably muted atmosphere of the room, "I heard ya boy didn't make it home last night." "Nah, he didn't," I replied, shooting Danny another funky look of disgust. I sat there staring a hole into his soul. "Sis, focus on me. Right here Sis. Hey. Sis. Come on. Come back. I'm right here," Ben beckoned. Finally, I released and turned slowly back to my brother. "There you go," he said, with a soft voice of reassurance mixed with a sigh of relief. He too knew how I had grown to let my temper get the best of me during times of heightened frustration. So, neither he, nor anyone else with any good intentions for our marriage, want to see me go off; especially not when things had gotten this deep, and most certainly not in my current condition.

"Sis, I just want you to know I believe him. I really believe he's telling the truth." I looked at him like he was crazy with a smirk that said 'negro please' on my face. Yet he continued, " No Sis, I'm serious. You know I don't uphold him in his bullshit. But this is some different stuff right here. I'm for real. I was there last night when he asked for the pain pill. Remember, he agreed to lay off the powder. So now he's feeling that back pain again. So, he asked for a pain pill. Becky gave it to him and said it was a Lortab, but I found out later it was a Klonopin. I was wondering why he was so out of it. 20 minutes later he couldn't even hold his head up straight. He was drooling and everything. I told them he needed to go home, and she volunteered to take him. I figured he would be ok. I didn't know it was going down like that though."

I sat there a bit shocked, but still angry. "You mean to tell me she did this shit on purpose?" Ben replied, "Apparently so." I was furious. I went on to tell Ben, "You know your boy don't do good with Klonopin. Right?" He said, "Yeah, that's what he told me."

During our years of drug use, we had a time in which we did a lot of pill exploration. During those times, we discovered Klonopin turn him into a zombie. As high as his drug tolerance was, those were like his Kryptonite. There was no bringing him out of it either. It just had to run its course and wear off. Still, I didn't feel like this justified his idiocy in allowing her to give him a pill and him not paying attention to what he was taking. With that, I held on to the belief that he set himself up for that. But this chick though. She was a whole other level of low down. I asked Ben, "So you mean to tell me this bitch drugged and raped my husband?" He looked at me with all the sincerity and disappointment in the world, "Apparently so. That's

23

exactly what it looks like."

I hit the fan…inside though. My thoughts of what to do to her to exact my revenge ran as wild as ravening wolves. All I could think of, in a rational sense, was, "Thissss bitch. This motherfucking bitch.' Then, I found myself saying it aloud, "This trifling assed, dirty, low down, no good assed bitch." As I repeated various versions of the same song, Ben sat there waiting. He knew my wheels were turning because my brother knows me. He was sitting there holding my hand, without a doubt, waiting to see what I was going to do; which direction I was going to go in. What in the world was I going to do? They both HAD to wonder, because they knew me all too well. There was no crime that went unpunished when it came to my husband. But that night I completely surprised both.

I gathered myself and all my frustration. Once I was able to collect my thoughts I said, "Thanks for coming by and clearing that up for me Bro. I'm tired though. I'm ready to go back to bed." Ben looked at me; puzzled to the max. He had no idea what had just happened. None. He looked at me. He and Danny looked at each other. Then he looked back at me and asked, "Sis…are you okay?" I said, "Yes. Of course." He tightened his grip on my hand and pulled at it ever so slightly looking me square in the eyes, "No. Sis, are you okay?" Me, "I said yes." Still, looking at me intently he came again, "Sis, are you SURE you're okay?" I looked at him square in the eyes this time so he would know I was not lying to him, "Bruh, yessss. I'm fine. I promise. I'm just tired. I'm tired of him. I'm tired of them. I'm just tired. We'll talk more tomorrow. Okay?" "Okay," he replied with a raised brow and look of concern as if I needed to be admitted to the ICU. He and Danny continued to exchange looks; very concerned looks that tickled me so bad I couldn't help but giggle.

I said good night to Ben, then Danny saw him out the door. I could hear him thanking Danny for coming through to clarify things as best he could. I also heard Ben tell him how much he hated this, and that he hoped we could work through this. Then I heard Danny say he hoped so. To me that was the biggest joke of the night. Danny hesitantly came into the room. He was obviously nervous, and for good reason. He had no earthly idea what I would say or do. At this point, every move made him increasingly more nervous. I hadn't flown off the handle yet, and that was not like me at all.

It was later that I learned from him that he would have felt better if I had just cursed him out, threw things at him, hit him, or done whatever else an angry black woman in living the housing projects had a reputation for doing at the time. But that one the things I was taking into consideration. Those reactions had never solved anything before, and they surely wouldn't solve anything at that time. In all honesty, I felt it was too good for him and a waste of my time and energy. The last thing I wanted to be was predictable. That was letting him off way too easy.

He slipped into his bed clothes, then looked at me solemnly and asked, "Is it safe for me to go to sleep?" I giggled at the sound of the fear in his voice and said, "Yeah, if you think so," then turned over laughing to myself. They had no idea. I was going to fix him and her. One way or another.

WHISKEY BOTTLE BANDIT

One evening, Danny and I were sitting home drinking. At the time, it had become a regular thing. Even though the drug use had ended, the alcohol continued to flow like water; honestly, it was much heavier than before. During that phase in my life, my mother would tell me it seemed like I stopped doing dope only to replace it with alcohol. In a lot of ways, it was true.

We both went from being high all the time to being drunk all the time. At the time, we felt like it was a step in the right direction. Maybe. Maybe not. Still, it was self-destructive behavior. It only had a different face. That, I know for sure. That evening, we had decided on a half-gallon bottle of brandy. As the night progressed, so did our intake.

I have no idea why, but when I would drink it was like giving me a Red Bull. I could go all night long. The more I drank, the longer I would stay awake. We both had a habit of drinking ourselves to sleep. The only difference between he and I is, he would regularly drink until he blacked out completely, with no memory of the day or evening before. In blacking out, he would snap. His eyes would change, and so would his attitude. He turned into a completely different person. He would get angry and want to fight; which is what happened this night.

We were in the room drinking and cutting up like we usually did, when he began "the change" while we were hanging out in our bedroom. I was all too familiar with it. I learned to see it coming. So, me being me, I said, "I'm not doing this shit with you tonight. You can just stay the fuck back here. I'm going in the living room." He mouthed off whatever he was saying in his drunken stupor. At that point, I wasn't even paying attention to him. He was killing my buzz. But I was determined to get some peace. I grabbed my laptop, headed to the living room, and sat in my designated corner of the sofa.

I stayed in my little corner of the sofa, leaving only to pour more drink. Then, from the back bedroom, I heard him rustling. He was tossing things around talking crazy; yelling through the door. My response was, "Okay man. Whatever. You just make sure you stay the fuck back there, and I'm going to stay the fuck in here, and we are going to be ok." He kept yelling through the door. "Fuck you motherfucker. Stupid assed bitch." My response, "Like I said, you can say what the fuck ever you want to say, as long as you stay the fuck back there and leave me the fuck alone." Apparently, cursing me out wasn't good enough. He just HAD to fight. ...again.

Mind you, at this point in our relationship, I had grown tired of fighting. In my twenties, I didn't mind a good old-fashioned bar room brawl or one-on-one knuckle-up. I would throw blows and hang with the best of them. ...men included. But I had three children; three sons. They were old enough to see and know what was going on. They were no longer at ages where they could easily forget traumatic happenings. They were at an age where things stuck with them. Taking this into consideration, and the fact that my heart was somehow changing, I tried to minimize the fighting. But once he blacked out, there was no going back until he finally passed out.

Then the door opened. I sat, rolling my eyes, slowly leaning my head back, finally looking up at the ceiling. He was coming. And there was nothing I could do to stop him. One way or another, he was going to get his fight. I just thanked God the boys had decided to spend the night at a friend's house.

I stood up and looked past the kitchen to the bedroom door, "Man go on, dude. Just turn the fuck back around and take your ass back in the room. I'm not up for this shit tonight." He just stood there staring like one of those zombies off the walking dead when they are in their calm state. Again, "Man, listen… I ain't up for this shit tonight dude. Just go back in the room and go the fuck to sleep." And again, he stood there. After staring back at him for a few seconds, I shook my head and sat back down with my laptop.

Slowly, he exited his room and made his way past the dining area looking all grim and evil. "Man, listen. I need you to go back in the room. I'm in here minding my own business, not bothering you. Just go on now." He began to mumble under his breath things I can't tell you because I really don't know what he was saying myself. When he acted that way there was a demonic air about him. It seemed as if he were completely possessed. In a way, I guess he was; possessed by alcohol.

I knew this; he was coming for a fight; just like he did every other time. I tried to remain as poised as possible as he approached, but he finally got TOO close and stayed there. He was standing over me as I was working away at my laptop waiting for my slow internet connection to load my next page. "Dude, you need to back the fuck up man."

But he stayed. "Bruh, I'm telling you. I need you to get the fuck out from over me. I told you I'm minding my own business. Just go back to the got damn room man!" But he stayed, standing over me, staring down at me.

Me being me, I finally had to make a stand. It was too much. He was too much. I sat my laptop to the side on the sofa out of harm's way. I rose to meet his eyes, then look down on him as my height slightly dwarfed him. "Man, I told you, you need to back the fuck off me. I'm in here minding my own..." and there we were; locked up. I don't know who grabbed who. All I know is we were at it again. I was so sick of it. But what choice did I have?

Into the chair we went. Around the room we went. Then, there was the coffee table. This time, there was no safety glass. This was real, old-fashioned paned glass. One of the favorite tables I had owned. I crashed through. He landed next to me. The pain shot all through my body, but my back and the back of my leg required special attention. I thought about the pain, but I didn't have time to nurse it. I had to defend myself.

'Concentrate on the fight girl. He's coming back,' I thought to myself. And, as usual, he wasn't feeling any pain. He rolled over and went for his infamous choking position. I was there with him alone, and I knew if he managed to choke me until I passed out, he might not stop and I night not wake up. Not by "intent", but he had blacked out. He had no idea what he was doing. He rarely ever remembered the next day.

As he was pressing his hands around my neck, I remember being very tired of these antics. I hadn't wanted to fight him in the first place. I had been there before, in that same position; just in a different location and a different home. The time before, I had fallen backwards and hit my head on the kitchen cabinet's handle. I had been lucky it had only put a nasty knot on my head instead of gashing my head open.

During that fight I had managed to lean forward far enough to bite his lip. He had snatched away while I was still biting down and ripped his lip open. Still, with his lip splayed open to resemble the Predator, he continued to sit on top of me and choke me. Thankfully, yet unfortunately, our oldest son was had awakened. He tried to coax him off by yelling his name and telling him to stop, but he wasn't going. Our boy was eventually forced to place him in a choke hold and drag him off me. That was a really sad and low point. Still, that was a whole other fight in a totally different place. As you might have gathered by now, we fought a lot back then.

At this point, I was willing to do what it took to get him off me. Everything short of killing him. I didn't want him dead. But I did want to live. So, what to do? Then, I saw a glimmer of hope. The half-gallon brandy bottle we had been indulging in lay on the floor. I can only imagine it landed there after being knocked off the table during our struggle. But it was perfect for the purposes I needed it for. Unfortunately, it was just out of arm's reach. So, I pushed harder. I remember struggling to get it thinking 'I really need this before I pass out.' I continued to reach thinking, 'Just a little further'. And I reached, 'My God, I'm not going to make it.' Just then, the rounded neck rubbed the bottoms of my fingers. That seemed to give me just the right amount of extra energy I needed to extend my arm. Finally, I managed to roll the neck of the bottle into my hands.

Ding! I remember the sound of the bottle as clear as day. It still had a bit of brandy in it, so the sound wasn't completely hollow. I heard it and he seemed to have felt it, but he didn't stop. It seemed to have only pissed him off more. Ding! I beaned him again on the top of the head. He still held on tightly. Ding, ding! Once to the side and once to the back. He finally began to reel from the effects of the bottle having been rapped over his head repeatedly. He fell back into the floor yelling, "You fucking bitch! You dirty motherfucker!" It was something how, as long as he was doing what he was doing to me, things were ok. But as soon as the tables turned, I was everything but a child of God.

I can remember how he had his family under the impression that I was dogging him out and doing him wrong. It took his brother coming for an extended visit to witness the chaotic mess the boys and I were forced to deal with living with him day after day. It was only after he gave his eye-witness account of the madness that they finally believed their "poor boy" wasn't so much a victim after all.

He clamored his way up off the floor, stumbling back into the room. I sat there in the floor dazed and trying to catch my breath. I shook my head, trying to regain my composure; looking around the room to assess the damage. The living room was destroyed…again. There was broken glass everywhere. Blood drops trailed from the living room floor, through the kitchen and dining area, and into the bedroom.

I was furious as I thought to myself, 'All I asked him to do was leave me alone. Just stay in the fucking room. But no. He just had to come out with this shit again.' Then, from the back room, he called in a weak voice, "Vykki. Vykki." I sat there still furious, and even more offended that he would have the gall to call me; with a pitiful voice; as if I would want to cater to any perceived need that he would have at that moment. I pulled my legs under me and got to my feet, stumbling back toward our master bedroom, "What the FUCK do you want? Whyyyy the

FUCK are you calling my GOT-damn name you SORRY piece of SHIT assed motherfucker?"

As I approached the room, I could see his legs sprawled out just past the threshold of the doorway. My thought to self was, 'You have got to be fucking kidding me!' But I continued, "What do you want man?" He answered, "I need you to take me to the hospital." It jarred me, this bold request of his. I said, "Wait a minute. What?" He responded, sounding pitiful and helpless, "I need you to take me to the hospital." Off the handle I flew, "Are you fucking KIDDING me? You come in here starting shit, putting hands on me and you want me to take you to the hospital? Even if I wanted to, I couldn't. We've both been up drinking all night. I'm not going to jail for your dumb ass. Stupid motherfucker. If you want to go to the hospital you drive your GOT-damn self!"

Danny continued to lay there, hand on his head, bleeding on the carpet, groaning in pain, "No. Seriously. I need you to take me to the hospital." I replied with adamancy, "You should've thought about that shit before you decided you wanted to fucking fight. You drive yourself to the hospital. Or lay there and die for all I fucking care. I'm sick of your shit." I stormed back into the living room, pissed to the highest, and sat on the sofa with my laptop. I guess it was my attempt at gathering myself. I don't know. I do know I was surrounded by debris and broken glass. I remember looking across the room and seeing the brandy bottle laying there on the floor, covered on one side with blood. I let out a singular, "Hmph" under my breath, and commenced doing whatever it was I was doing on my laptop.

I heard him finally rustling around in the room on the other end of the house. Then, suddenly, I heard him on the phone, "Yes, I need an ambulance. This bitch is trying to kill me." In my mind, 'What the FUCK?' Then, my mouth, "WHAT THE FUCK?" He yelled, "Yeah bitch. Your ass is going to jail." I sat there listening in disbelief as he told the dispatcher on the other end that I had assaulted him, hit him in the head with a giant bottle repeatedly, and wouldn't take him to the hospital. He went on to say he had passed out in the floor and woke up in a puddle of blood; and that he was still bleeding.

At that point, I really did want to kill him. He had the audacity to instigate that entire thing, and when he got his tail handed to him, turned and played the victim. I was LIVID! If he had dropped dead, I wouldn't have felt bad at that moment. I felt like he SHOULD die; that our family would be better off without him. But for him to blatantly lie on me to the authorities…that was a whole other level of bull!

Danny made his way outside with the phone and stayed on with the dispatcher until the police and ambulances arrived. Soon enough, there accumulated in my yard a record number of police. Before, they only sent one or two cars when the neighbors called them. But this time, the drama king managed to beat them all. A whopping five cars and two ambulances, all with sirens blaring, swarmed the little acre of land we were in the process of purchasing.

I sat on the sofa waiting patiently for him to finish feeding his lies to them; watching through the large picture window as they attempted to interview him. I remember being tickled at how a couple of them gave each other crazy looks and scratched their heads as he spoke. I have no idea what he said. I just know whatever it was didn't help his lies and his obviously drunken state.

Finally, as they brought two medics to check him on the front porch, two officers made their way to the door of our mobile home. "Ma'am, are you okay?" the female officer asked. "As good as I can be given the circumstances." She asked if they had permission to enter. I said yes, and they stepped in. They asked what happened, and I explained the events that had unfolded through the night.

The male officer said, "You said you hit him with a bottle." I replied reassuringly with the most serious of looks and emboldened attitude, "I sure did. He was going to get his ass off me one way or another." Both he and the female officer looked at each other and exchanged a look of '…well.' The female officer continued, "Ma'am, since this is a domestic violence case, they brought me in to check you for scars and bruising. Is that okay with you?" I responded, "Yes, that's fine." At that, she and the other officer began to look me over intently. I didn't think anything of it. However, they had a LOT to say about it. And what they had to say brought me into a reality check; a perspective I had never had before. It was one that changed my life forever.

THE SAGA OF THE FRONT DESK CLERK – ACT 3

Over the next few days following Danny's night out escapade, I was slow to speak and very cautious in what I said and how I reacted to him. Never in my life had I acted with so much fake function and resolve. But at the time I felt it was necessary. I WOULD have my day. I didn't care what came or went. Hell or high water, I was going to pay him and Becky back for what they did to me.

I presented myself the complete opposite of the way I felt and thought. I put on a stellar performance that was easily Oscar-worthy. The only other person that had a hint of what was going on in my mind was Tasha. That is because Tasha KNEW, knew me. She knew I wasn't going to sleep on that level of betrayal. She was just waiting patiently for my play to reach its closing act so she and I could lavish in the fullness of my story of sweet revenge. I was all too eager to make it work, and had no it would work so well. I'm not saying what I did was right. It was not, by any means. But still, in hindsight, I even impressed myself.

I slowly worked my way into pretending I forgave him for his foolish folly. "No babe, it wasn't your fault that bitch drugged and raped you. She needs her ass whooped.

But I'm going to chill and act like I don't know shit. Then, when I drop this load, I'm gonna get that bitch." That was the great historic tune I sang day after day, and it didn't sit well with him at all. He hated when I said that, "...drop this load," as if my baby was a giant turd waiting to be expelled into the sewer. Still, I said it just to rub him the wrong way. ...a minor irritation. Nothing to let on where my mind really was with the whole scenario. And the "raped you" part burned his butt to no end. And I mean NO end. Still, I would sound off with the same song over and over again.

We both hated fake people. If you can't do anything else, at least keep it 100. That was supposed to be our shared belief. But, in my book, that no longer applied to me. Not in this case. Not with her. This scenario made she and I exceptions; and he hated it.

Danny hated the fact that I insisted on acting like nothing ever happened in front of others. On the rare occasions that I went by the tattoo shop, I made it a point to be cordial to her. I played stupid and friendly all too well and he hated it. But he didn't understand how necessary it was. He thought I was waiting on the opportunity to just beat her up after I had the baby. I could do that and not play stupid or fake. But he had no idea. My determination for vengeance ran much deeper than he could fathom. I had to play it by ear. Somehow, someway, they were going to be repaid. Then, a few weeks before Christmas, a series of events were sparked by an unexpected catalyst; the gift of giving.

Apparently, Becky's conscious had been getting the best of her, and she was being overly nice to Danny; asking about myself and the boys, "...making sure we were okay and that the baby was okay." She knew I was on bed rest, supposedly for the fullness of three months, until our third little on had come to term for safe delivery.

When he came home and told me of Becky's inquiries and attempts at tattoo shop conversations, I laughed in amusement. That part was real. It was, quite possibly, the only real emotional reaction I had toward him until the day I exacted my revenge. He would get angry and say, "The shit ain't funny. It's not funny at all." But to me it was hilarious, and he hated how much I acted as if I was completely unbothered by it; the fact that he was forced to work with the woman who raped him; the fact that I asked him to continue working there; to do it for the family because the shop money was going to eventually get us out of the projects and bring him enough revenue to finally invest in his own spot. He hated it; and he hated her. But he did it for us; to get us out of the projects. That much I will give him. He did want us to have a better life.

Becky, with her extra bold self, out of the blue decided she wanted to get into the Christmas spirit. Oddly enough, she decided to include my family. When I say a guilty conscious speaks, sometimes it does more. Sometimes it yells. Sometimes it screams at you uncontrollably. Sometimes it drives you stone crazy. Sometimes, when you refuse to apologize or own up to your wrongs, you attempt to buy your way into paying penance; especially when you feel like you didn't get found out, and you want to keep your secret buried deep, but you still want to make amends. Guilt can be heavy and detrimental to your health.

Becky asked Danny to bring me and the children to the shop because she had surprises for us. As much as he hated her, he knew that there would be no rest until she had gotten her way. She tended to be persistent, and no matter how many times he instructed he not to talk to him, she insisted on trying to converse with him anyway. At least that's how he described it.

Danny came to the apartment and made the announcement, "Hey Babe, Becky wants me to bring you and the boys up to the tattoo shop. Her dumb ass went and bought gifts; toys and all kinds of shit." I was insulted as hell yet tickled beyond belief. "Really," I asked. "That bitch really is crazy. Ain't this some shit? But I'mma be crazy right with her ass. Let's go." He shook his head in disappointment, knowing I was going to go play the role. My goodness he hated it. But I felt it was necessary. Very necessary.

We arrived at the shop and were greeted at the door by Becky and her bestie. As we walked in music was playing in the background, holiday décor had been placed here and there, and there on top of the display case was a pile of neatly wrapped presents. Becky hugged my neck, "It's so good to see you! Oh my God, you look great! And look at you glowing! Oh my God! And the boys! My goodness, they are so big!" She carried on with the compliments and greetings as her bestie echoed her antics and agreed in the background. Finally, all the hugging and smiling and fake reception of their unwanted "concern and love" was over, and I could stomach myself a little better.

As I took a seat in the waiting area, she began to explain to me her reason for requesting I leave the comfortable bed my doctor had assigned me to. "I know you've been having a hard time being on bed rest and all. So, I wanted to do something for you guys and the boys. I know it will make it hard for you to shop like you want to, so I wanted to do something special for y'all. I hope that's okay with you." I replied, "Oh that's perfectly fine! Thanks so much for thinking of us! You didn't have to do this! This is all just so sweet of you!" She just didn't know. In my mind I was thinking, 'Bitch, I will take ALL your money; and a whole lot more than that. You just wait. I'm going to fix your ass.'

However, instead of expressing my true feelings, I turned to the boys, who were then only three and eight, "You hear that boys? Becky has Christmas presents for you!

They thoroughly enjoyed unwrapping their gifts and placing the batteries in to give them a go, completely unaware of the numerous problems in the room. They both received remote control vehicles and a few other toys. But the R/C cars was most memorable for them because that was that they loved; cars.

The thing with Becky is, she didn't stop there. She turned to me and said with excitement and a smile, "I hope you don't mind. I got something for you and Danny too! It's not much, but I wanted to get a little something to let you guys know I was thinking of you." At that moment, I remember having the hardest time not laughing in her face. I could have laughed her into the floor; literally into the floor. Instead, I stayed in character like a good player should. I didn't want to ruin the game.

I delivered my performance flawlessly, "Awww! You shouldn't have! Thank you so much! You are entirely too sweet!" She presented two beautifully wrapped boxes; one to me, and the other to Danny. As we opened them, I could see the angst in Danny's face. He was not into it. But I didn't give a furry little rat's behind. I continued to coax him to play along with my little game. After all, it was only until I had the baby. Right? And at that point, his disillusioned seat of forgiveness and peace was where he wanted to stay.

Danny opened his box and I opened mine. Inside the quaint little black boxes were two necklaces. His had a snare drum with sticks crossed, and mine had musical notes on it. They were both sterling silver and as cute as can be. I thanked her profusely for all the gifts, and Danny even managed to muster up a, "Yeah, thanks," grumble under his breath. But Becky... Becky had to keep pouring it on. She said, "I'm so glad you guys like them! Come on! Put them on! I want to see you in 'em!"

Just when I thought the scenario couldn't get any richer, it did. I hope the Lord doesn't punish me for this, but it still cracks me up to think of the look on his face. Danny was so sick of her it was ridiculous. He looked as if he was in physical pain attempting to keep himself together. He fumbled with the clasp as he tried to close the necklace behind him. Seeing this, Becky volunteered, "Here, I'll put it on for you." She looked at me, "May I?" I responded, "Of course!" She went on, "That way you don't have to get up any more than you have to with the baby and all." My gut flipped from laughing so hard on the inside as I watched Danny cringe while she carefully latched the necklace for him.

That day, I believe I laughed more than had since before that entire experience began. It felt good. Honestly, it felt too good for me to relish in the anguish of my ex-husband and play Becky for a complete and total fool. And to think, that was only the beginning of my conquest for revenge.

SO, YOU LOVE HER MORE

We decided to separate, but I let him borrow my car to go do some tattoos. After all, he had been the sole bread winner, and I needed money to care for the children. Soon after though, I got word that there was a young white girl riding around town in my whip. Of course, with me being the hot-tempered chick I was back then, I wasn't about to let that fly. So, I asked my mom to take me to his spot to pick up my car. When I arrived, my car was nowhere to be found, but there he was; looking crazy and as high as a kite. So, I went in raising as much hell as a hellraiser could raise. An argument ensued, of course, and his roommates went about their business as usual. This was nothing new to them.

The lie he proceeded to tell was that the girl was supposed to use the car to go get cigarettes and come right back the night before, but hadn't returned. He went on to say they weren't fooling around. She was our homeboy's girl. Well, ok. But why didn't homeboy take her for smokes? Why didn't she use his car instead? It made no sense. But with him nothing ever did when he was up to no good. His lies were just that. Lies. Excuses to make himself feel better about doing what he did. Funny part is, I watched him fictionalize scenarios and stick to those stories until he believed them himself. Life was wild with him. Sometimes, I even questioned myself and others around me to be sure I wasn't the one tripping'.

So, he called girlie to have her return my car, but she didn't answer. But I wasn't leaving without my whip, so I told my mom to leave and I would handle it from there. So, I waited. And as I waited, he asked for money to buy some powder. Of course, me being the addict I was at the time, I felt I needed something to calm my nerves, so I pulled my money and made the call.

Eventually, my guy delivered. It still trips me out to think of how excited he got over the fact that the little round white package had arrived. Ain't that something? It disgusted him to see me coming, but when I was holding a bag of blow, he almost salivated at the sight; not of me, but of Snow White. She was so much more beautiful to him than I. Never would I have imagined, when I first married him, that he would love something else so much more and hate me so viciously. Still, I didn't realize the extent of his disdain until a few moments later.

Just after my delivery, he got the call. My car was back. When I proceeded to approach the door, he issued strict orders for me to stay in the house because he was handling it. I was taken completely aback by his demand. I knew at that moment the girl was much more than our homeboy's girl. Otherwise he wouldn't be protecting her because he knew I was going for her. So, like the idiot I was, the obedient wife despite it all, I sat and waited.

Shortly after exiting the house he returned with my keys. I got excited because I just wanted to go home. I just didn't realize getting those keys back wasn't going to go as smoothly as I thought it would. Not even close.

When I held out my hand for the key, he said, "No. Give

me the bag." My reply was, "No, it's my bag. I haven't even had time to hit it yet." He started heating up immediately and cut me a stern look that let me know he was ever so serious about this business, "Give me the bag Vykki." "Hell no," I replied. "This is my shit and those are my keys. I'm not giving you my shit and I haven't even had any yet." So, I proceeded to walk into the bathroom to hit a couple of bumps. Of course, he followed.

Me being the ornery person I am when I'm irate, I wasn't going to give him anything on his terms. It was mine. I paid for it with the little money I had made. And I was going to give him what I wanted him to have. So, I scooped him out a bump and attempted to hand it to him. Man, that really pissed him off. "Give me the fucking bag Vykki," he said with an angry growl in his voice; eyes burning with rage at this point. My response, "No. You need to give me my keys and take this bump because this is my shit and that is my car." Apparently, that wasn't the best idea because he grabbed me and the bag in my hand and there we were; wresting over a stupid little bag of cocaine worth $25 in the front bathroom of someone else's house.

We tousled for a while until he pulled one of his trusty moves, he learned in the Marine Corps. I found myself halfway in the bathtub and halfway on the floor, gazing up at his fist drawn back in the air ready to strike. I gave in and let go of the little plastic baggie. He finally had what he wanted; this white girl he loved so much more than me. He finally got her, and he was happy.

It was only then that he threw my keys at me and let me know, "You stupid assed bitch. That's why I hate your ass. That's why I don't want to be with your ass. You always trying to control shit. When you gonna realize you ain't shit? You don't control shit. I RUN THIS SHIT. BITCH YOU AINT SHIT. I run this fucking shit! When I get back your ass better be gone. I came here to get away from your stupid ass, so you need to get the fuck out." He stormed out, followed by the rest of his friends that had been there waiting outside the bathroom.

I heard the footsteps as they exited the front door. I sat, still slumped in the floor, partially laying over the side of the bathtub staring at the toilet. Don't ask me what was so amusing about the toilet at the time. I believe I had to have something to focus on in order to maintain my sanity and keep from flipping out. I still felt it coming though. And I knew it was going to be bad. I just didn't know how bad. The anxiety attack was on its way. All I could do was pray.

I slowly crawled across the floor. I will never forget the feeling of being so humiliated, not realizing at the time things would only get worse. By the time I made it to the threshold of the bathroom door I was beginning to gather my footing. The floor was cold and I felt so weak. I wasn't hurt too bad. Not like I did after the usual fight. So it wasn't that. But my heart. It was my heart. As I tried to comprehend what had just happened, a million thoughts ran through my mind; including my heart. I didn't want to die. But my heart…

See, we had separated so we could work on getting better and being better for each other. At least that was the impression I got. But clearly this was not his goal. It was another lie. But instead of just saying it in the beginning, he took the coward's way out. Then, I let him use my car to work so he could help me with the children. But that was a whole other lie. He just wanted to do what he wanted to do. Damn me and the kids. And this lil white girl he had riding in my whip couldn't have possibly been just a tattoo client. Tattoo clients don't get to drive my car. And last, but most certainly not least, this negro put hands on me and drew his fist back at me over a bag of cocaine; a twenty-five-dollar bag of cocaine!

All those thoughts and emotions ran through my mind at the same time. And to think, this used to be the love of my life. I was his everything and he was mine. We loved like no others had loved. We were in sync to the point where we finished each other's sentences and held full conversations with our gazes. How did we get here? At what point did we take a turn for the worst? I could see if it were someone else. But something else was just something else entirely. Some THING else. That other white girl. Snow White. It kept playing in my head, "So you love her more than me? You love really her more than me."

Never had I ever known true heartbreak before that day. I have heard of people dying of broken hearts, but never thought it could happen to me. But here I was, trying to gather my strength to get off the floor. I saw a broom across the room, so I walked over to it slowly. Dragging my feet along the way, I made it. For some reason, I felt I needed to move. I felt that if I didn't make myself move, I would just die. I already felt like the process had begun. My chest was tight. I couldn't catch my breath. I tried to focus my thoughts so I could calm down. But it just wasn't working. I remember thinking at one point, 'Oh my God. I'm going to die here. …alone. And it's probably only going to piss him off even more; to die at the spot and draw police and detectives. He would be so angry.'

But I kept pushing. I started sweeping. From one side of the room to the next, I attempted to keep moving and focus. But my heart… It just wouldn't cooperate. Every time I lost control of my thought flow a fresh tightening would come, and I would feel myself weakening again. I was so afraid. SO afraid. I found myself standing in the middle of the room, clinging to the broom handle, praying for the Lord to let me live. Please don't let me die here.

45

Not like this. Not alone. Please.

I held on tight, praying, but sliding slowly down the broom and into the floor. I finally gave in. I prayed and prayed. If I died, then so be it. There was nothing I could do. I had prayed and it was now in the Lord's hands. As I settled into the fetal position on the cold hardwood floor, I finally managed to breathe. My chest finally unlocked. The unrestricted air was so refreshing. And to think, I just knew I was dying from a broken heart.

I finally gathered myself and the little pride I had left. I stood in the middle of the floor, scanning the house slowly, thinking of all that had transpired within the last hour or so. Then, that's when it hit me. The acceptance, the anger, the bitterness, and the new attitude. No more of the brittle, bruised, and delicate emotions. That tender girl melted away in the pile of tears on the floor. I clearly remember the thought to myself before I said goodbye to those timid tears, "So you love her more than me. Huh? Fuck it." Then, as I walked away from the tender timid tears, I walked out of the door a changed woman with a new attitude.

THE SAGA OF THE FRONT DESK CLERK – ACT 4

Shortly after our little Christmas encounter, Danny went to jail. He was made to sit there for quite a few weeks. In the meantime, my dad moved into our extra bedroom to help with the bills since Danny was the only one able to work at the time. Though Danny was his least favorite person in the world, my dad was willing to do what it took to help me through a safe pregnancy and make sure the boys were taken care of.

During that time, I had also learned that one of Danny's co-workers and good friends, Brandon, was single. He was tall and quite handsome, did lots of cocaine, drank a lot, and was known to be a womanizer and an abuser. He was perfection for the task I chose to implore him for. I wanted him to date Becky and boy did I get my way. It only took a couple of weeks for things to take off. As a matter of fact, she moved him in so quickly it even made my head spin. But things fell into place perfectly.

It wasn't long after Brandon moved in with Becky that I started receiving feedback about how she would show up to work bruised and disheveled. I relished in every moment of every detail. She allowed him to come into her home, and word on the streets was that he forced her to pay for

47

his supply, cursed her like a dog, and beat her repeatedly; leaving only body marks as to not give himself away too easily. It was crazy, but I loved it. And my little birdies loved keeping me informed. They knew what had happened between her and Danny, and after all the public humiliation, they were more than happy to oblige when it came to instigating drama between Brandon and Becky so they could come back and tell me of more pain and suffering he had caused her.

With the stresses of all the chaos that was going on, my contractions got to a place where they were no longer subsiding with my medication. My friends and family knew of my situation, and it took no time for the word to get to Becky and Brandon that Danny was in jail and I needed help getting around. So, with her usual overly interjective self (and I believe a little coaxing from Brandon), Becky volunteered to take me where I needed to go.

Well, you know I couldn't pass up the opportunity to use Becky. After all, she owed me big time. So, I took her up on her offer, and planned to milk her as much as I could before my little play came to an end. She seemed as if she was more than happy to oblige, so she became my transportation to and from my doctor's visits.

One day I went in to be checked, and the doctor was overly concerned that the breathaline was not working. There, she laid it out on the table, "If you want to hold this baby to term, you have got to go somewhere that is stress free. No children. No husband. No dad. No nothing. You will need to find a place to stay, maybe with a friend, until you reach at least thirty-six weeks. No sooner." This was week thirty-two. Only two more weeks to hang on. As much as I didn't want to be away from home, I knew I didn't have a choice.

Again, Becky jumped at the chance to be of assistance, "She can stay with me! You can stay with me! It's only me, my boyfriend, and my son. And he's older, so he won't be a problem. He will be able to help me take care of you." I was so tickled on the inside I could barely contain myself. My thoughts to myself were, 'This bitch has really got to be ape shit crazy! I am going to worry the living shit out of her!' But my outward character stayed intact, "No! I couldn't possibly let you do that! That's sweet of you, but you've already done enough!" She replied, "No. I insist. I really want to do this for you. Come on girl. Let me do this for you." So, I did.

I arrived home and gave my dad the doctor's report. He agreed that I needed to do what necessary to make sure the baby came into the world healthy and strong. So, I packed my things, kissed my two little men, and hopped into the car with Becky. We pulled down her long driveway lined by forest on either side, then came to a massive clearing that opened to reveal a beautiful and spacious one-story home with vaulted ceilings and a full attic. She was glimmering with excitement and bragged about the architecture of the house; how it had been customized by her ex-husband, and how much freedom, space and peace I would have during my stay.

She had called ahead, so Brandon and her son (pardon me for not remembering the poor child's name) met me at the door to help me into the house and gather my bags. Brandon, sweetheart he was to me, took me gently by the arm and guided me from the truck into the house. Becky's son was instructed to gather my bags, and so he did. We took a little time to tour the house so I could know where everything was located. This was, by far, the hardest part for me. I walked through knowing this was the place where she'd had sex with my husband. The place where she had supposedly raped him while he lay unconscious from the pills, she had given him.

The living space was gorgeous. It was an open floor plan that joined the kitchen with the dining area serving as the middle. There was a long prep counter with a built-in cutting top (one that this girl living in the projects envied quite a bit at the time), and beautiful custom cabinetry that wrapped two walls, then came around to a finish under the countertop.

Down the hallway to the left was her son's bedroom, the shared bathroom, and the guest bedroom I would be sleeping in. To the right, at the end of the hallway was her bedroom door. I don't know why, but for some reason she saved that room until last. I don't know if she was testing the waters when she took me through there or what. But I do know that room struck a nerve in me. With that, I took care to "hold my mouth right" as the old folks say here in Alabama. Into her master bedroom I went.

She showed me her California King bed with the beautiful hand-carved hardwood posts that my ex-husband had given a vague description of when he tried to recall the events of that night. As we moved across the room and into the master bath, I was able to identify the rounded garden tub Danny described being in; not knowing how he had gotten there; only remembering someone running water over his dreadlocks in the tub. Then, there was the giant window. He remembered a giant window. There was, indeed, a window directly in front of the bathtub.

She was on private property, so there was no one to see into the bath. Only the animals in the forest. She went on to explain how she loved to bask in the sun when she bathed, and how beautiful it was to soak and watch the deer play in the back yard as she burned her candles and sipped her wine.

I found myself fighting off random thoughts of doing her physical harm as I played on like a good player should; never breaking character. It was only on the way out of her room that I almost lost my composure. As we exited to go back to the living room in search of books for me to read, I noticed a brown tee shirt. I knew that tee shirt. That was my husband's shirt. Instantly I went bananas in my head, 'You mu-thu-fu-kin BITCH!!! You really did rape my fucking husband! He's been looking for that fucking shirt! And, of all places, it's laid across the foot of your got-damn footboard! BITCH!'

Beyond pissed is where I found myself. And what happened in response? I began having contractions. I grabbed the bottom of my big belly and said wearily, "Girl, I need to lay down. These contractions are kicking in again. From there, she escorted me back into the living room. There, I lay on the sofa doing my cleansing breaths to ease my repetitive belly aches. Finally, I was able to settle into a good book. That was the beginning of my stay at Becky's Manor.

☐

WHISKEY BOTTLE BANDIT – PART 2

The female sheriff's deputy and her partner looked me over thoroughly. She did most of the talking as she informed me step-by-step of what she was doing. He stood by with the camera, ready to snap pictures as she instructed. He snapped pics of my head, my face, my neck, and my arms. She turned me around to inspect further then paused for a moment.

When she broke her silence she said, "Ma'am, I need you to step into the restroom." I looked at her kind of crazy like 'What the heck for?' To my facial expression she responded, "Ma'am, you've been cut. There is blood on the back of your pants along with a huge gash in your pajamas. I need you to step into the restroom so you can pull your pants down. Is it okay if I bring a medic in with us?" I said, "Yeah, that's fine." Between the mixture of adrenaline from the fight and the numbing effects of the alcohol that had yet to wear off, I hadn't noticed the pain; though I would feel it all later.

We entered the front bathroom as a group, and I proceeded to pull my pants down. She leaned down to examine my injury and said, "Ma'am, you are going to need stitches." I looked at her and responded, "No. I'm good. I'll be fine," wanting to have nothing to do with them, let alone a hospital. She insisted, "Ma'am, that is a nasty cut. And it's going to leave a nasty scar if you don't get stitches." I looked at her and insisted, "Ma'am, I will be fine. It can't be any worse that any of the other cuts I've had before. I just want this to be over with." She shook her head but still replied with a sigh of disappointment, "I understand. I need to take pictures of this for your case file. Then, you will need to fill out a statement. You will just be writing down everything you have told us. Ok?" I agreed.

When she had done all, she was going to do, I headed back toward the living room. She turned and said, "Ma'am, I understand you're tired, but I'm going to have to ask you to step outside to talk to my superior and file your report." I stopped and looked, then replied, "No ma'am. I'm not going outside so I can be arrested for public intoxication." Her partner replied, "No ma'am. It's not like that. It's just dangerous for all of us to be in here with the broken glass all over the place. That, and the chief wants to talk to you. He's going to help you file your report. That's all. We're not trying to entrap you. You seem to have been through enough in one night." I remember being so nervous. But what could I do? I had to file the report. If I didn't give an official statement, there was no telling what they could charge me with. So outside I went.

As we moved through the doorway, I remember the medics having Danny laying on a gurney still checking him. As I walked past, I couldn't help but stare at him. I grilled him with a look of contempt that made them somewhat nervous. They beckoned to me, "Ma'am, don't look at him. Just focus on us. Focus on us. We're going right over there to the chief's car."

One officer in the front, the other into my rear, I was

escorted slowly and carefully from my home. My goodness I was so angry. Still, I didn't want to seem noncompliant. That was the last thing I needed with this negro telling them I had tried to kill him. As we proceeded past, I could hear the medics speaking to Danny rather aggressively. Evidently, he was giving them a hard time and had gotten them frustrated. Not surprising to me at all. This wasn't their first rodeo with him either. Two calls had been made to them in those recent months, one of which had been Christmas Eve, for his self-induced alcohol poisoning. So he was not a stranger to them.

We made our way across the yard to the chief and his car. He started questioning what had happened, and I found myself repeating the story. ...again. By this time, I was irritated and tired. The alcohol was beginning to wear off and the pain was starting to kick in. During the conversation I had to interrupt him, "Sir, I know we've got to do this, but could I please sit on the back of your car. As you well know by now, I'm good and drunk. Now, I'm hurting and wobbly. I need to sit down, please." He obliged and helped me hop up onto the back of the vehicle. As I went through my story again, he proceeded to flip through the pictures the deputies had snapped inside.

He stopped abruptly and said, "Wait," showing me a picture of the bloodied brandy bottle, "You hit him with this?" I answered, "Yes sir, I sure did." He looked at me with a lifted eyebrow and asked again, "Ma'am, you hit him with this big assed bottle?" I repeated my confirmation. "Okay, go ahead." After what seemed like an eternity, I finally finished recounting my experience for the second time and writing up the account on paper for formal filing.

The deputies asked what to do next. The chief checked with the medics and asked if they were taking Danny in. They insistently said no, and I knew precisely why. Again, that wasn't their first rodeo with Danny. Both times they were called out in the past, he had tried to fight them when he came around. In one instance, the doctors at the hospital didn't even want to keep him because he was so belligerent. They were, by no means, fans of his.

With the medics response, the chief said, "Book him for domestic." The male deputy working the case proceeded toward Danny to take him into custody. The female stood there looking at the chief. He looked back. Then she broke her silence, "What are we going to do with her?" I could have come unglued. She was really standing there waiting for the opportunity to book me. I couldn't believe it! The only female officer on the case, and she was willing to book the victim too. That was an unbelievable moment for me. Sadly, it wouldn't be my last unbelievable moment as a domestic violence victim. Still, I had to maintain my composure. It was up to them whether I went to jail with Danny.

The chief looked at the female deputy and answered sternly, "She is the only one of the two I could get a comprehensive conversation out of. He is the only one being belligerent. I'm not putting her in jail. Besides, somebody's got to be here when those kids get home from school." Then, he looked at me and nodded, "Thank you for your cooperation ma'am. Get you some rest and try to have a good rest of your day." I thanked him, then proceeded to the house.

Inside, I looked around at the mess that had been made. I was too exhausted to bother cleaning. I snuggled up on the sofa with the bloodied bottle of brandy, poured myself the last few drinks, and cried myself to sleep as I felt around on my body, inspecting all the bruises and wounds the deputies had shown me on their handy little camera. As I drifted into my drunken sleep, I recalled their speech about how I was lucky to be alive after having gone through that glass table. I could have died from being impaled. I could have died from being impaled. I could have died from being impaled. Sleep found me quickly as those words echoed.

I awoke late in the afternoon; much later than I wanted to. I had planned to have the tornado of a mess cleaned up by the time the children arrived. Unfortunately, I was just getting started when the bus pulled up at the end of the driveway. The children made their way into the house. I made it a point to greet them with the biggest smile I could give and directed them as best I could. Of course, they wanted to know what happened. I explained loosely that we had accidentally broken the table. Then they asked where their dad was. My answer said everything they needed to know. Dad was in jail and the house was smashed. There was another fight. Being the sweet boys, they are, they obediently stayed in their room until I managed to remove all the broken glass and get the floor vacuumed thoroughly. Sadly, with their dad gone, we could experience peace. We missed him, but not the drunken crazy him. We missed the good husband and good dad. None of us realized at the time we would never get that guy back.

Later, Danny's boss called and asked about him. I informed him that he had been carted off to jail again for yet another domestic violence charge. As much as he hated when Danny got in trouble, Danny was too valuable to his business for him to let him stay in jail. He asked repeatedly if I would get him out. I repeatedly answered no, not that time. Enough was enough.

Finally, he called me to his home for a meeting. He, his wife, and a couple of his helpers had a round-table meeting with me concerning Danny. They were willing to put up the money for his bail, but he would have to come straight there and agree to very specific terms for paying them back and continuing to work. I stood firm on my no until they brought the boys and my bills to the table. At the time, I didn't work. I handled the paperwork for the tattoos and the sub-contracting for our art company. Their overly valid point was, the boys needed their dad, and I needed him out to keep up with the bills. That was all true, so I took the money and headed to the jail to post his bail.

I hated being at the jail. It was almost a regular thing, and they knew my face. It's bad when the Sheriff and the jailers recognize you. That was recognition I had never wanted to earn. Still, I was back again. Bailing him out...again. I waited out front for what seemed like an eternity. The door from the back opened and closed, opened and closed. Then, finally, a big burly man came out, escorting Danny. Looking in my direction, he laughed and said with his deep southern drawl, "Well, if it ain't the Whiskey Bottle Bandit!"

A look of curiosity spread across my face. He couldn't have possibly been talking to me. Maybe I missed something. So, I turned to look around behind me to see who he was talking to. But there was no one. He laughed a hearty laugh and continued, "No ma'am. I'm talking to you darlin'. You've earned yourself a nickname, young lady! We decided to call you the Whiskey Bottle Bandit!" He laughed and laughed as if it was the funniest thing in the world. He had no idea how infuriated and embarrassed I was. Not only did they recognize my face, I now had an official nickname, compliments of the sheriff's department by way of Danny.

Again, I found myself livid. I went from zero to one hundred in one-one-thousandth of a second. I couldn't believe it. And as angry as I was, I only wanted to crawl into a hole and hide. I did not want to be bothered with Danny either. He had broken my peace on too many times. I was officially sick of him and his antics. Still, I could not just drop him like a bad habit. There was business to be handled, and I was part of that business. We had children to raise. And still, I loved him. So, away we went.

A few weeks later, we were required to appear in court. That was one of the most humiliating days of my life. The judge knew us all too well. She looked at Danny and said, "You again. Huh?" She then looked over at me, "And you're still with him. Huh?" She looked down at the case file, then examined its contents carefully. She looked up at the sheriff and questioned him, "So she hit him with this?", holding up the picture of the bloody bottle. To this, the sheriff answered, "Yes ma'am, she did." The judge proceeded, "And why wasn't she taken into custody?" The sheriff answered, "Well, your Honor, she was the only comprehensive one at the scene, and we could tell he was the aggressor because he was problematic for the paramedics that tried to assist him. She was also the only one that could tell her story straight and consistently."

The judge rolled her eyes, then looked at Danny, "She might keep bailing you out, but you are going to do something different this time." She went on to sentence him to anger management classes, alcohol restriction, and color code. She finally looked at me, "Ma'am, you seem like an intelligent young lady. But if you keep dealing with this mess and bailing him out there's got to be something wrong with you." I was sick behind her words. But she was right. There was something wrong with me. When I left that day, I was bound and determined to fix it.

THE SAGA OF THE FRONT DESK CLERK – ACT 5

The first evening of my first stay at Becky's house was an awkward one. She had over a few guests, and I joined in the laughs as they congregated at the dining room table. I was served dinner at what came to be my comfy spot on the living room sofa, and they all sat around eating. Becky's son was taken aback when she announced, "Y'all, this is Danny's wife. She will be staying with us until it's time for her to have the baby. Per the doctor's orders, she needed to get away from home to a comfortable place that is stress free, so she won't going into labor."

Her son jumped up from the table yelling, "What? Are you serious?" She looked at him, then me, then back at him with a look on her face like the cat that swallowed the canary. I could tell she hadn't expected him to react so abruptly at the announcement. I immediately realized the kid knew something what she had done, and previously had no idea who I was. She spoke calmly to him, "Son, sit down. Don't do this. She is our guest. Don't be rude." He stood over the table looking at her with burning anger, then stormed away to his room.

From my seat on the sofa I asked, "Is he okay? Is there a problem?" Brandon chimed in, "What's his problem?" He was completely oblivious to the fact that she had taken my husband in her bedroom before the two of them became an item. She finally responded with a fake smile, "I'm sorry y'all. You know how teenagers can be. They can be funny about their space. He's just not used to me having company. He'll be fine." I knew that was a lie. The kid knew something, and I was curious to find out what.

Over the next few days, Becky's son warmed up to me, and turned out to be just as sweet and helpful as he could be. At one point, when he was bringing me my dinner he

59

said, "Here you go. I'm sorry about all this." He shook his head with disgusted look, lowered it, and walked away. I didn't inquire. I just ate. I knew he knew something. Whatever it was, the poor child held remorse for what his mother had done. That, I believed, was the saddest part of it all. I didn't know at the time just how sad the situation really was until the very end.

As I settled into my stay at Becky's lovely home, I made it a point to be as needy as possible. I began to get on her nerves, and I knew it all too well. She and Brandon would argue in the mornings before he left for work, and she would emerge from her room acting as if she was still happy to help me. I knew she was ready for this to be over, but she had volunteered, so she had to stick it out; per Brandon's orders. And that, she did.

Finally, the day came that she took me to the doctor and we both received the good news we had been waiting for. Even though I was a couple of days shy of thirty-six weeks, the doctor believed the baby was far along enough to have a safe and healthy delivery. At that point, she was more worried about the long-term side-effects the breathaline would have on his health. I agreed with her wholeheartedly. After having read the side-effects, the long-term effects had been heavy on my mind. So, I left on a mission to deliver.

In preparation to go to the hospital, I made Becky aware of the fact that I had no items to take into the hospital; no gown, no slippers, no period panties, no shower caps... everything I could think of, I named. We went shopping and she footed the bill. I picked up everything I needed and some. I was completely void of remorse as I racked up on comfort items and ran up her credit cards. She tried to make me aware of her "budget", but to that I paid no mind. I "needed" those things.

Hesitantly, she purchased it all. I laughed on the inside as I put her through the pain of running past her budget. I could tell it was taking a toll on her pockets. Still, I cared not.

No sooner than Becky and I arrived back at her house, I began to have contractions. My breathaline had worn off, and the contractions were moving well. My doctor had given me strict instructions to stay away from the emergency room if possible, and to only go in when my contractions were regularly at least three to five minutes apart. Anything less, and they would send me home with more breathaline.

As we were grabbing my bags preparing to leave, I asked, "Hey, where's Danny's shirt?" My thought processes were to let the baby smell his dad's shirt so he could know his smell when he was released from jail. But that later sparked an idea that would set up my jackpot move for payback. She happily obliged and assured me that was a "fantastic" idea.

Taking into consideration the fact that I wouldn't be allowed to eat until after I delivered, I informed Becky that I was hungry, and I wanted a delicious wholesome last meal before officially becoming a mother of three. She informed me that she had tapped out when she took me shopping earlier in the day. I whined a bit and put on my face of disappointment. The puppy dog face worked. She finally gave in, "Well, I have a couple of gift cards we can use at the Cracker Barrel." I lit up with excitement, "Great!"

We exited the house, she loaded the bags, I got comfortable I the car, and off we went. Soon, we were at Cracker Barrel, and I was ordering the biggest meal I could find. So much so, she ordered a small plate for herself and sat, watching me scarf down my pre-delivery meal kicking one leg straight out from under the table as I rubbed my huge belly with each contraction. Finally, the timing of my contractions was just right; and they were perfectly timed with my last bite of food. Becky sat eagerly waiting. The time of her penance was almost over, so she thought.

Upon arrival at the hospital, we learned the doctor's plan had worked. I was admitted to the hospital to deliver, not be given more breathaline shots and sent home. Becky and I were both filled with excitement about the baby coming. I believe this was the only occasion I celebrated with her that was genuine. She stayed as I gave birth. My parents had yet to arrive, and everything happened so quickly that they didn't have time to make it for the birth itself. The doctor joked that I had almost delivered on my own. My little bundle of joy came with no complications, and he was perfectly healthy aside from his low preemie birth weight. And Becky snapped very tastefully done pictures of the delivery, and newborn pictures of him to take to Danny.

Suddenly, it hit me. "Becky! Where's the shirt?" I was so excited! The idea that popped into my head was going to make him go ape crap crazy. Becky retrieved the shirt from my overnight bag. "Put it on," I said. She stopped and looked at me like a deer caught in headlights. I could have peed myself laughing at the startled look on her face.

Becky hesitated, "What?" I responded, "Yeah! Put Danny's shirt on! Little man will smell his dad on you if you put his shirt on. I want to take pictures of you holding him!" It looked as if the life drained from her body as she stood there trying to process my request. I knew then I had to hurry up and make it happen before she backed out and ran off. I insisted, "Hurry! Put the shirt on before he gets hungry and I have to start nursing him again." She slowly slid the shirt over her own and walked toward the bed. There, she laid the camera at my side, and I handed her my little bundle of joy.

I took the camera with all the excitement in the world, "His dad is going to think this is such a great idea! He is going to be so happy to know he was able to smell him even though he couldn't be here! You are so sweet for doing this!" She looked like she could have died right there, and that thrilled me to no end! I relished in the moment, but she was antsy and somewhat obvious about the shirt thing. I could tell it was creeping her out, and to me at the time that reaction was golden.

I was in my own heaven watching Becky squirm. Still, she managed to muster up a smile with my little man in her arms. I snapped away; determined to capture the perfect pictures to share with Danny. The woman I believed he had an affair with, the same of which he accused of raping him, was wearing his shirt posing in his stead with his newborn son. He would die inside, and I knew it. Quite frankly, I was eager to watch him fall apart. But, just as this had come in time, so would that moment.

During my stay in the hospital, I had my mother take the photos to be developed. On my way home from the hospital, we picked them up. Once I was home, had spent time with my boys, and had gotten settled back in, I got back to business. I sorted through the pictures carefully, only picking the best ones that told the story of our son's birth. After all, Danny had missed it, so I wanted him to take in a much of the experience as he could with the photos. I strategically placed Becky's pictures at the end of the stack. He needed to see those last. I remember having carefully planned to crush his spirit once it was at its height. The proud daddy would have his pride obliterated as soon as it bubbled up to its fullest potential.

Per tradition, my mother was in place to help me around the house and with the children when I returned from the hospital. Soon enough, I was able to convince her to allow me to borrow her car to run the pictures to Danny at the local jail. She hated the notion. Where I'm from, we are taught a woman is not supposed to do anything other than tend to the baby until her six-week recovery period has expired; not even drive. But Mom knew I was one that always went against the grain, so eventually she said yes. But I was to come right back. I agreed, and happily drove across town to the jail.

The jailers were stunned that I was out. I explained that I was only there to deliver the pictures. They were kind enough to allow me back to Danny's cell, where I handed him the stack of pictures with a smile on my face that could have been compared to the fat cat on Alice in Wonderland. I stood, talking to him about how fat and handsome our little man was; waiting for him to get to the pictures. I watched and chatted, patiently waiting as he slowly made his way from one picture to the next. He was so proud of our little handsome man. I could tell his heart was just bubbling over with joy as he spoke about getting home soon to hold him for the first time. Then, it happened.

There was no mistaking Danny had finally made his way to the pictures of Becky wearing his shirt holding our little one. I could have exploded with sinister laughter as I watched the light sink out of his eyes and the glow drain from his face. I could literally feel his joy being snatched from him, and his pride dying. It felt good. It felt way too good.

Slowly he tried to gather himself, "What the fuck, Vykki?" I stood looking, trying to maintain my composure; hanging on to my role just a few seconds longer, "What babe? What do you mean?" He looked at me with an angry fire in his eyes that tickled me so deeply down on the inside that it felt like my soul was even laughing and I would pop soon if I didn't let it out.

He responded, "What the fuck is THIS SHIT, Vykki?", turning the picture toward me aggressively as he spoke. Just then, his eyes fell on yet another pose of her holding our little bundle of joy. "Are you fucking kidding me Vykki? You fucking kidding me? Why the fuck does she have on my shirt? Why is this bitch holding my son?"

At that point, I couldn't hold it any longer. I laughed. My God knows I laughed. I laughed until my belly hurt. All he could do was stand there staring at me. I believe if he could have gotten his hands on me, he would have. Instead, he was in the perfect place to be contained and an even better place to have nothing to do all day but allow those images to burn into his mind. Perfect.

Once my laughing fit ended, I was more than happy to explain how I used her as my cabby and financier during the course of his incarceration. I also told him of how I relished in the luxury of her cozy home, used her and her child as my personal servants, and even had her purchase all my supplies for the hospital to ensure my stay was as comfortable as possible.

I went on giggling throughout the explanation at my ability to play the whole game improv, "When I saw your dumb ass had left your shirt in her room laying across the foot board, I knew I had to make it work. So, I told her to wear the shirt so baby boy could smell you after his delivery. So your first time seeing your son, you get to see him in the arms of the bitch you had an affair with; the one you hate so much that you claim raped you; wearing your shirt from that night, standing in for you in your absence. Aren't they just adorable? Didn't she do a good job? I knew this shit was gonna be good. But it ain't just good. This shit is fucking golden!"

He stood, trying to comprehend everything I had just

told him. Looking into his eyes, it seemed as if he was trying his best not to lose it. He looked at me, "Vykki, this is some bullshit." I continued to laugh. He went on, speaking very low, "This is some evil fucking shit Vykki." I responded matter-of-factly, "Did you really think I was gonna just let you do this shit to me and do nothing? You fucking crazy?" He interrupted, "This is some evil fucking shit Vykki!"

I kept on, "You really thought you could publicly humiliate me, have me stressed slap the fuck out, have people walking around looking at me with pity motherfucker, and I wasn't going to do anything about that shit?" He tried to introject, "Vykki…" I stopped him, "No. This is what you get. You get to sit here until you get released and marinate on that shit. Day after day, you get to think about the fact that the bitch you claimed raped you, the one you had the little tattoo shop affair with, was the same bitch that held your son for the first time. Not you. Her. That bitch. Sleep on that motherfucker." I exited the police station with the biggest crap-eating grin on my face and my heart smiling. Mission accomplished.

I left the police station satisfied with my sweet revenge. Becky was living with a man that beat her on a regular basis thanks to my keen hand at love connection. I understood she was too afraid of him to make him leave, so it would be a while until those beatings stopped, and I was completely content with that. Danny, on the other hand, had to live with her being at his child's birth in his absence. As much as he loved his boys, I knew that would eat away at him; if not forever, for a long time to come. Unbeknownst to me though, the saga continued behind closed doors.

A few days after I delivered my perfectly placed photos to Danny, Brandon came knocking frantically at the door. I could not, for the life of me, imagine what was going on.

My mom called, "Vykki, there's a strange white man at the door." We both knew a white man in those projects was a rarity. I knew then, it had to be Brandon, and it had to be serious because he didn't come there unless he was buying his supply. Even then, he didn't come to my place because my place wasn't the place for that; at least not at that time.

I walked into the living room, where the door was open to the screen door to allow some light in. I waved my hand and said, "Come on in Brandon." I continued to introduce him to Mom. She spoke and went back to her business in the kitchen. He was looking so desperate to me it was concerning. He looked at me with all the seriousness in the world and said, "We need to talk." I replied, "About?" He said, "I don't want to talk here. But this shit is important. I've got some shit I need to tell you." I looked at him like 'What the heck?' He said, "Listen, I know you are supposed to be in the bed. But this shit is important, and I can't have this conversation in front of anybody. We need to talk in private." I saw the conviction and desperation in his eyes. I gave in, "Hang on, let me get some shoes on."

I went to my room, put on my shoes, and grabbed my knife. He was my boy and all, but people that are creatures of drug habits tend to be unpredictable sometimes; and with the way he was acting, he was making me nervous. I came back out of the room and made my mother aware that I was stepping outside to talk to him. She nodded her head, and off I went. I asked, "So what's up?" Brandon responded, "We can't talk here either. Your neighbors are nosy as hell, and I left my truck parked around back. You know they'll rob the shit out of a white boy over here." I agreed, and we proceeded to walk around the backside to the basketball court.

Once we reached the side of the building, Brandon finally opened up, "She fucked Danny. Becky fucked

Danny!" Before I could think about it, I laughed. I mean I was bawling laughing. He stood there with a look of shock on his face. He finally broke, "What the fuck Vykki?" I tried to answer, but I couldn't stop laughing. He asked, "You knew?" I shook my head yes as I continued to laugh. My poor friend. He was so angry. "You mean to tell me you knew this whole fucking time?" The more he inquired the harder I laughed. I finally had to stick my index finger up, in my signed request for him to give me a minute because his reaction to the discovery was cracking me all the way up and I couldn't contain myself.

When I finally caught my breath, I explained to Brandon that I had known all along what had happened and how I played both Danny and Becky by ear for their deception and lies. Brandon followed carefully and agreed with my actions as I went through the story step-by step with him. In the end, he was proud of the way I had handled things. Still, he felt it wasn't done.

He explained, "I told that bitch she's gonna apologize to you." I tried to talk him down, "Nah, bruh, I'm good." I got what I wanted out of her. I used her as much as I felt like it. I'm good." He said, "Nah, sis, you don't understand. I already told her I'm gonna beat her ass every day until she apologizes to you. And I meant that shit." At that point, I realized how serious he was. He was not playing about his little sister. He really was going to keep beating her.

I finally said, "Fine. Ok. Tell her to call me." He said, "Oh hell nawl! You're going with me. She's at the house waiting. I told her I was coming to get you." I replied. "Hell nawl! I'm not going back to that bitch's house. I got everything I wanted from there. Not going back." Brandon pleaded, "Come on Sis. Just ride over." He continued to go back and forth with me until I finally gave in.

After reporting to my mom that I would be making a

quick dash, Brandon and I hopped in the truck. Off to Becky's we went. Upon arrival, Brandon beckoned me to go with him. That was a no go. I told him I wasn't going into her house, and I wasn't playing. With that, he went in. I heard some yelling from my passenger seat in the truck, then they emerged from the threshold of the door.

Brandon appeared with Becky by her hair, dragging her along. She tried her best to keep up, but she was barely making it. He finally got her to the passenger side door of the truck where she stood crying uncontrollably. He pulled her hair back and looked her in the face, "Don't you have something to say?" She stood, crying, face red, "I'm sorry." I just sat looking at her. He pushed her in the middle of her back toward the truck, "Tell her!" She repeated, "I'm sorry!" I cocked my head to one side and asked with the utmost attitude, "Sorry for what?" She looked a bit puzzled at my question, so I repeated it again, "Sorry for what? What the fuck are you sorry for?" That was when I got way more than I could have ever asked for from my maliciously improvised game.

Becky spilled the totality of her innards through her barrage of tears, "I'm sorry for what I did to Danny. He asked me for a pain pill, and I gave him Klonopin. I was supposed to be taking him home, but I didn't. I brought him home. I got my son to help me get him out of the car, and put him in my bathtub, and bathe him, and put him in my bed. Please, you can whip my ass if you want to. I deserve it. Please. Go ahead. Beat my ass. I know I deserve it."

I was in shock by how she admitted \ having involved her poor son and confirmed that she had, in fact, raped my husband. At the same time, I couldn't help but laugh because she told it all without a clue that I was partially aware of what had transpired. As I sat there laughing in her face, she managed to stop crying. Her look changed to one of complete bewilderment. I explained to her through my laughs, "Stupid assed bitch, I knew the whole time."

Once again, the color drained from her face. I continued, "I knew the same day he came home. I just didn't let you know I knew. I played your ass the entire time because I was going to make sure your ass paid in full for the fucked-up shit you did to me and my family. You really raped my fucking husband, you desperate dirty, low down assed bitch. But that shit you pulled with your son, that's some really fucked up shit. Your own child. You put your own child in the middle of this shit. You deserve whatever the fuck you get. But what you won't get is the satisfaction of this ass whipping you know you so rightly deserve. My hands are too good for that. My hands are too good for you. I'm satisfied knowing you've got to live with the shit you did, and that you got played the whole time you thought you were in the clear. And besides, I hear Brandon has been whipping that ass well enough anyway."

Turning to Brandon, "Brandon, get this bitch the fuck out of my face and take me home." He asked, "You sure you don't wanna give her that ass whipping?" I answered, "I'm positive." With that, Brandon left her where she was, walked around and hopped into the driver's seat, then pulled away. She stood there, seemingly in shock, watching the truck as it left her beautiful sunlit yard.

A few months later, I ran into Becky on the sidewalk at the store. I had heard she was strung out bad, but I hadn't realized she was almost zombie bad. I had also heard she was going crazy. But that one of those things that happens when you must live with the guilt of your wrongs. Still, in a way, I couldn't help but feel sorry for her because she looked to be in such a bad state.

I acted as if I didn't see her, but I caught her eye and

she called out to me, "Vykki." I stopped and looked at her with the fullness of the attitude I carried for her. She walked over cautiously, "I just wanted to let you know that I really am sorry for all the stuff I put your family through. I really am. You can still whip my ass if you'd like. I know I still deserve it."

Before I knew it, I was laughing again, "Girl, didn't I tell you these hands were too good for you? You should feel bad for what you did. You deserve whatever shit you're in and whatever else comes." Then, I proceeded to get into my car and pull off, leaving her standing there, once again, speechless and unforgiven. That would be the last time I saw Becky. And I didn't miss her a moment.

The next time I heard of Becky, she was dead. Apparently, she decided to commit vehicular suicide with another passenger in tow. It was almost a year to the date after my Danny didn't come home.

THEN GOD CALLED

After a long drawn out road of domestic abuse, drug abuse, self-loathing, chaos, and confusion, something happened. I knew a shift was happening in my life because I was trying to change. I was trying to do better. I was trying to work with Danny to do better; to get better together. But Danny wasn't having it. I had made up my mind that I was going to do what I needed to do for myself and my children with or without Danny.

I began to pray and seek God. Even in my drunkenness, I knew He was my only hope. I found myself reaching back into the faith I had once abandoned in a desperate plea for help. Much like the prodigal son, I was coming to myself, and I remembered the goodness of my Father's love.

When I couldn't reach Danny, I would pray instead of cursing him like a dog. I had grown tired of the fighting, and I knew after so much experience fighting would do no good anyway. The only thing I knew to do at that point was pray. I had been talking to my spiritual leader on and off at the time. He was kind and patient, and so was his wife. They would both accept my 3am drunken calls after I had a falling out with Danny. They would speak kindly and patiently, and pray with me with the hopes of helping us with a breakthrough.

My mother would invite me to church, but I had such disdain for the church institution and the people in it I continued to refuse, time after time. She would always say, "You don't go to church for the people. You go to church for God. ...to be fed." I heard her, but I wasn't hearing her.

Finally, one day she said again, "I want you to go to church with me." I jerked my neck, looked at her with my nose upturned, and gave my usual answer, "I'm not finna be foolin' with no stuck-up holier-than-thou church folk." She replied, "I already told you, you don't go for the people. You go for God. It's not a regular service anyway, it's a women's conference. It's on a Saturday, and we have all kinds of fun stuff planned." She kept on about all the plans they had made, and the cute little blue hats they had designed; all of which made me that much less interested in attending. Finally, I caved, "If it will make you happy and get you off my back I'll go. Oh my God, I'll go!" Despite my nasty arrogant attitude, she jumped with excitement. I regretted it as soon as I had agreed.

Then, the big day came. I had stayed up drinking heavily the night before, so I was tired and hung over. I was hung way over. But I had to go. If I didn't, I would never hear the end of it. I showered and bathed in body spray. Still, I knew that I would reek of liquor from the previous night. With that, I decided to sit in the back of the sanctuary, and just make minimal contact with all the "church-folk."

I arrived a bit late, but I could see a look of sweet relief on my mother's face as I entered and took my seat in the next to last pew. I sat quietly as I watched each person play their part; the soloist, the special guests, the words of encouragement, the special activities...

Then there was the women's discussion panel. It was almost painful to listen to them as they seemingly spoke from the pages of my life. It was like the questions posed to the panel, along with the answers the panelists gave, were taken directly from my life and the recent struggles I had been dealing with. I was in awe.

My soul wept from the truths that were being spoken about my circumstances. I was sitting there facing so many of the harsh truths I needed to hear. At the same time, I was being reminded of the many teachings I had learned so long ago before I rebelled against the church and against God. With each passing moment of the conference, I felt a crushing; a breaking even. But it felt good. It was like I was being broken so I could be opened and emptied out. Little did I know, that is exactly what was happening in the spirit realm.

As I sat on that second to last pew, for the first time I heard myself; my own voice in my head, ministering to people through word and song. I had no idea where it would lead me to. I learned a short time after that it was God revealing my future to me. I was being called. I was receiving my own prophecy.

The longer I sat and listened, the more restless my spirit became. I found myself crying with pain and relief all at the same time. I tried to compose myself, but the tears just wouldn't stop. Then to add fuel to the fire, the minister that was the speaker of the hour brought a message that touched me to my core. I found myself hanging on her every word. Every portion of her message was relevant, and it was good.

No matter how hard the truths were to accept, I knew they were truths that I needed to hear. Not only that, but they were truths that were giving me life. And I hadn't felt that alive in a very long time. Before it was all over, I knew.

What did I know? I knew I had a purpose. I knew that my life was meant for more than being a drunk. I knew that the Lord had delivered me from being a drug addict for a reason. I knew that, just the way he delivered me from my drug addictions, he would deliver me from being a drunk as well. I knew I worth more than I had been giving myself. I knew I was worth more than I had been allowing myself to take. The abuse had to stop. The madness had to stop. I was meant for an abundant life; not a disastrous one.

I knew that day that God designed me with a purpose and that day He was calling to me. He finally had me in a place where I could hear His voice, and He was calling to me. I heard Him clearly. His voice was unmistakable. I felt knew within myself if I didn't answer the call I would walk back out to a defeated life. A life where I was totally lost to the world with no guidance and no hope.

The conference was nearing a close. Time was running out. But I didn't want to stand up in front of all those people; all those judging eyes; all those people that knew me for what I was. Then, my mother's statement came to mind, "…not for the people. …but for God." And just as they were closing comments, I raised my hand.

The hostess beckoned me to stand. I didn't know what to say. I was a jumbled mess, but I let it out. I opened about how much the activities of the day had blessed me and let them know that it had inspired me to come back to the church. I even offered up my services as a singer. I admitted how I had realized, as much as I had sung for the world and in the streets I now realized that my gift had not progressed because I was using it everywhere except where the Lord intended for me to use it. At that moment, I rededicated my life and voice back to Yahweh God; to whom it belonged.

During that service, God spoke to my spirit. God called

and I answered. That was the beginning of my journey in to healing; my kintsugi. Going forward from there, I didn't realize how rapidly the Lord would progress my spiritual healing. But every time I turned around, He was blessing me in another way. Every time I looked up, He was making a way for me to be delivered from another place of frustration and bondage in my life. Slowly, but surely, I witnessed the Lord take my broken pieces and mend them back together.

All the hurt and pain from my past began to dissipate little by little. Sometimes, admittedly, it was painful; especially when it came to breaking ties with toxic people. Breaking old ties was comparable to detoxing from dope. It hurt. It was challenging. It was frustrating. At times, I even wanted to go back. It was hard to keep away from people and things that had been so familiar for so long. But guidance from the Word of God and the fortification I received from His Holy Spirit made it much easier to cope.

Once I got past the initial pains and shocks from the processes, I felt so much better. I felt brand new each time I was finally able let go of someone or something else. I learned what it meant to be taken from faith to faith, and from glory to glory. Was it an overnight process? Absolutely not! It was a process that took time.

That's the thing about having been broken so many times; repeatedly. Mending takes time. It takes care. The more broken you are, the more fragile you are. The more fragile you are, the more care must be taken in your handling. Careful handling requires patience and time.

A fact that many of us are not aware of is that we do not have the patience, nor do we have power to mend ourselves back together; especially seeing as we aren't the originators of our own designs in the first place. But our Heavenly Father, the one and only creator, has the knowledge, patience, time, and ability to do it all; and do it for all of us.

When we allow Him to work in us, He will take all of our broken fragments, no matter how small, and carefully mend the pieces back together in His own magnificent form of kintsugi.

At this point in my life, I am single, happy, and quite accomplished. I have accomplished more since I answered the call of God than I accomplished in the entire combined span of my life prior to that day. In all essence, I have really only been living approximately six years. The years prior to that, I was merely surviving. There is a huge difference.

Out of all the wrongs I have done in my life, all the people I have wronged, the many sins I have committed, the abuse I have been subjected to and subjected myself to, and even the abuse I have, in turn, inflicted on others, God took my broken pieces and brought me to a place of wholeness. A place of peace. A place of love. A place of compassion. And most of all, a place of forgiveness.

Please understand that forgiveness is of the utmost importance. Unforgiveness is a toxic poison. It will consumes those that do not let go of past hurts and pains. That is why forgiveness was necessary to allow the Lord to make me whole again. There was no way He could work His great works in me if I had not finally emptied myself of all the hatred, remorse, and unforgiveness I was harboring toward Danny, Becky, and all the other people that hurt me so badly in the past. That unforgiveness took up the precious space that was needed for Yahweh God to fill me with His precious Holy Spirit.

The more I was able to forgive and let go of, the more room I had to receive the gift of His healing Holy Spirit. Just like the gold used in the art of kintsugi, the Spirit of the Living God poured into me; healing my heart; mending this broken vessel; filling me with His love, joy, and peace; allowing me to become more valuable and unique than ever before. Each of my beautiful, imperfect, glimmering, golden seams serves as a testament to the awesome healing work of my Father God, and I am here as a witness to tell the story of His goodness, His love, and His saving grace. My Father God and His masterful work of kintsugi.